MW01674459

Romance

Homosexual Group Sexual Encounters Involving Four Individuals, Specifically Including Men Who Can Transform Into Wolves, In A Romantic Context

(Supernatural Werewolves Fantasy Romance Featuring Shapeshifting Demons And Devils)

Juergen Hofmann

Van gazed into the parking lot through the glass. An elderly farmer was assisting a large, leather-clad man in removing a motorcycle from a horse trailer.

"You don't expect that kind of horse to be stepping out of a horse trailer." Parker sucked down a fifth of his Coke in a single breath after taking another pull on his straw.

Van occasionally felt jealous of Parker's rapid metabolism. Anything he wanted, in enormous quantities, could be eaten and never showed up on him. Van had to be careful with his diet, especially in the cold, or he would consume every calorie. Parker's one flaw was that he was almost always eating or drinking. He wasn't very fond of water, so he had to have some kind of soda, which became costly when they were traveling. Fortunately, Van's father allowed him to deduct the cost of feeding Parker from the business account because he saw it as an expense.

"What is your desired length of stay here?" Van shifted his feet a little and inquired. After spending over thirty minutes standing by the window, he was prepared to take a seat.

Parker scowled. "I suppose asking to stay here until the storm passes is too much to ask."

Van gave a nod. "Either of us has driven in worse. We could go the longer way, if necessary, but it would be preferable to loiter here all night.

Parker proposed, "We could go outside into the van and turn on and off the heater." "We're sitting down that way."

Many of the individuals in their immediate vicinity were finding places to sit in the aisles and wait it out, but some folks continued coming and going, spending time in their cars and then returning inside to warm up for a bit before leaving again. It was a choice. Van was also aware that Parker would require more food or go into a coma if he became too cold. That was one of the main worries when taking a hummingbird shifter across the highlands.

"I would much sooner return to the road. The path home is not that far away from us. Van was getting uneasy about the growing crowd inside the store.

"And how awful will that road be?" Parker's tone came out as nearly whiny to many, but it was just how he naturally spoke.

Van retorted, "That road is familiar to us both." "Everything will be alright." A deep breath left his mouth. "And when we're not around all these people, I'll be much more at ease."

Parker swigged on his soda once more. "There, I'm with you. Alright, when I use the restroom, let's grab me a few three-liters so we can head out.

Van gave him a narrow smile. "Gratitude."

"That's how buddies roll.Wemake concessions. Parker gave Van his cup. "Please hold this for me; I'll be back in a few minutes."

"All right." Van returned his focus to the parking area. There were more cars out there than there were people in the store, as far as he could tell. But that made sense given the volume of people arriving and departing. Wondering what had become of the man who had unloaded the motorcycle from the horse trailer, he cast a quick scan across the group. He hadn't noticed him enter. It was not a safe night to consider taking a motorcycle out. Van didn't want to even consider trying to ride a bike, even if he wasn't concerned about them getting home. Although he had only ridden a motorcycle once, during his undergraduate years, and in ideal circumstances, he had nevertheless encountered difficulties. It wasn't as simple as some folks made it appear.

Parker had vanished into the bathroom, and two men in bulky black coats emerged. They were clothed like civilians, but they moved like military types. As they made their way to the exit, they appeared to be observing every person within the store. Van felt a chill run down his spine as the closest one's eyes traveled over him. He wasn't sure what it was about the men, but there was something about them that bothered him.

"All right." Parker resurfaced beside Van. "Let me get some food, and then we can leave."

Van gave a nod. Alright. I believe I'll also pick up a bottle and some jerky. Just in case.

Parker shook his head, giving him a glare. "There is no just in case, dude. I will never forgive you if you mess things up and I end up almost freezing to death.

"Everything will be alright." Parker received his cup back from Van, and together they made their way through the trapped travelers, obtaining the necessary items to resume their journey. They wouldn't require any additional petrol, at least. With three quarters of a tank remaining, they could travel home and back to Aspen or Glenwood Springs.

Van inhaled deeply as Parker pulled up the collar of his coat and they stepped out into the storm. Van scowled. There were obviously a lot of hunters in the store based on the strength of the gun-oil scent, even if he hadn't seen many individuals who actually looked like hunters. The two men in dark coats might be an exception, but the others appeared to be travelers who had been caught off guard by the storm.

Parker pushed Van, "Don't drag your feet," as he dashed in the direction of the van. "Open up those doors." I'm chilly.

Van said nothing as he took the keys from his pocket and pressed the button to open the doors. A gentle click indicated by the locks springing open was accompanied by the lights flashing. Van lagged behind by a few yards as Parker moved to the passenger side of the van, slanting toward the driver's side.

Parker yelled, "Shit!"

Van's blood turned as cold as the wind striking his cheeks, and he decided to pursue Parker instead.

A harsh voice called out to him from behind, as the scent of gunpowder intensified. "Stop!"

As he obeyed, Van's heart was racing. The snow pounded his cheeks and his lips dried up.

"Remain there, please." The man trailing him inched forward, his position revealed by the slushing snow and ice beneath his feet.

Van questioned why nobody was leaving the store to assist them. It should have been obvious to anyone peering outside what was happening.

The still night was broken by a spooky wail. Van felt a chill run down his spine that had nothing to do with the man holding a gun behind him. He could smell the rifle and the man's eagerness without even having to see him. Van's stomach turned at the combination of the two.

Another man exclaimed, "I've got this one!" from the van's passenger side.

"Silence!" exclaimed the person behind Van. "This place has something more going on with—" There was a loud thud that interrupted the man.

The man was forcefully thrown into the rear of the van by a massive, gray object. It gave a loud rocking sound. Van pivoted. The man in the black coat was shaken by a big wolf. Van observed them for a little moment. Although he was accustomed to shifters, he had never encountered a wolf shifter. In Hardwood Valley, bears were the only big mammals that underwent shifts in their prey. He then bolted around the van in Parker's direction.

Parker wasn't there when Van stopped and peered down the passenger side of the van. In the damp snow were six packages of donuts and three liters of dew. "Parker!" he exclaimed.

An answer was not forthcoming. There, a vehicle roared to life somewhere nearby.

Van fled in the direction of the sound, just concerned about saving Parker and not about himself. Several of the other cars turned on their lights and fired up their motors around him. It was difficult for him to determine in the commotion whether one had fired up its engine first. He came to an end. After leaving its parking spot, a black Hummer drove toward the highway.

Van pivoted and bolted towards his van. He needed to trail the Hummer. Parker had to be over there. Just as he was about to reach his vehicle, the wolf emerged from between a Pathfinder and a Prius. It was almost as big as him when he was a bear. Its eyes were a blazing yellow, and its hackles were up. Van came to a stop and gave it some serious stares. "Look, my friend is with them." I appreciate the save, but I have to pursue them.

The wolf nodded, reached into the snow for a roll of something, and turned to face his van rather than Van. The wolf clearly wanted to accompany him.

"All right." Van dashed towards his car, the wolf trailing closely behind him. He took the man's gun, but he didn't even care to see if the dead man behind the van was okay. The firearm might come in handy, and he hadn't considered bringing one along for the trip. A few moments after the wolf settled down on the snow-covered footprints in the driver's seat, Van had the van in gear and the key in the ignition. Van had held the door open for the wolf to enter. He backed over the dead man with a painful thunk and moved in the direction where the Hummer had gone.

Van attempted to ignore the wolf that had crept into the rear as he needed to get to Parker and onto the highway before anything bad happened. The wolf killed a militarily trained man who, had he had the chance, would have killed him. Shifters going missing had been discussed in several of the shifter-only forums he kept an eye on for the community. He was positive they were carrying Parker, and he knew he would never see Parker again if he was unable to apprehend and stop them.

Malachai considered how he could introduce what he was going to do. But in the end, nothing existed. Johnny was going to be shocked by this, and there was nothing he could say or do to make it any less shocking. He had told him so much previously; now was the moment to demonstrate and provide evidence.

As a result, he drove home quietly than normal. His private beach stretch was tucked away from view by a natural incline that descended to the sand from the house. Unless they were on the beach or in the water, no one would be able to see him.

He had waited till it was dark for that reason. He should be safe enough as long as he didn't breathe fire or do anything foolish like that because there was little possibility that anyone would get close enough to see him.

It was a risk, by all means. Simply put, the risk was tolerable. That was what he needed to do.

Silently, holding Johnny's hand, Malachai guided him along the modest trail that went from his home to the small beach that was exclusively his. Ignoring that his jeans were getting saturated, he let go of Johnny's hand and proceeded to stand in the surf. They would soon be dried by the heat from his body.

He didn't take off his clothes. He was not required to. He'd heard that other shifters had to shred their clothes or remove them. However, dragons were a more ancient kind of shifter. deeper and more mystical. At least, that was what Malachai had always been taught. Naturally, he had encountered other shifters before, but he had never really spent any time with them.

Again, Malachai found it difficult to say anything to alert Johnny to what was going to happen. None were present. Johnny would just naturally find it hard to believe anything he said. Johnny was more accommodating than others, but even he had his boundaries. It appeared that there were some things that people were simply not meant to believe.

All well, there was no sense in waiting. Was this going to be the last straw for the camel? Could Johnny come to terms with this? Undoubtedly, discovering that information now was preferable to waiting until it was too late.

Who did he think he was kidding? It was too late now. Too little, too late.

He had no choice but to put his trust in fate and his partner. With that, Malachai inhaled deeply, transformed, and allowed the dragon to rule him.

This form has always seemed so friendly. For this reason, he would occasionally venture far into the forest and embrace his true nature. A portion of his identity. His true nature as a human was inseparable from that of the dragon.

Malachai was relatively small and skinny for a dragon, just as he had been as a human. His wings were tucked neatly over his back, and his scales, which matched his hair's hue, were a fiery red-orange. He ducked in, hoping that by making himself smaller, he would be able to prevent Johnny from becoming as frightened.

Even though it was small for a dragon, it was nonetheless massive.

Strangely enough, though, he didn't feel that his mate was very afraid. He felt amazement and astonishment, and yes, there was some anxiety, but not quite as much as he had anticipated.

"Malachai?" With Johnny's voice so faint in the darkness, Malachai turned to face his partner, whom he could see clearly. He could see every detail of his small partner as he stood and stared at him on the dry sand; even in his human form, he had greater night vision than most.

With a very quiet voice, Malachai answered, "Yes, little one, it's me." He could certainly growl loudly enough in this shape to be heard by most of Los Angeles, but he clearly didn't want that kind of attention.

As Malachai saw the human approaching, he realized he was correct about his mate. It was common sense for humans to flee from dragons; very few people would not do so. Perhaps Johnny was drawn to this place because he was his mate, or perhaps it was just the nature of humans. It was probably both.

Johnny muttered, "You're a dragon," and Malachai nodded with his enormous head. Apart than that, though, he remained still so as not to frighten his partner away. Johnny was handling things quite nicely and didn't want to spoil it.

When Johnny got as close as possible to Malachai's head, he seemed to reach out and touch his red foreleg. But his palm trembled, and he put it down once more, as if he weren't quite bold enough.

Alright, Malachai said, "I'm a dragon." And doesn't it all make sense? The infant, the mystique, and the magic.

After a moment of hesitation, Johnny nodded slightly, and Malachai had to force herself not to cry out in relief. There would have been nothing to be done but to wait for time to pass if Johnny had not come to believe even after all of this. If nothing else, Johnny's swollen belly would have served as proof.

But Johnny had been prepared to accept.

As softly as it was, Malachai prodded, "You can touch me," with a tinge of humor in his voice. "You can actually climb up and I'll take you on the ride of your life if that's what you want to do."

Malachai had assumed that since Johnny was a surfer, something along those lines would appeal to his adventurous side. He was also correct. For real,

Johnny smiled, stepped back, and turned to face Malachai.

Upon examining him closely, Johnny remarked, "You're sort of, well, huge." "How could I possibly stand up?"

Malachai lowered himself even lower and extended his front leg, offering it to lift Johnny.

He suggested, "Let your instincts guide you," understanding that a dragon's mate would have a touch with riding them that other humans wouldn't. In fact, Johnny had no trouble scaling Malachai's shoulders and settling into the open space directly in front of his wings.

Malachai urged the young one to hold on, and then, using his strong hind legs, he leaped into the night sky.

It was time to prove to Johnny that being a dragon's mate could be enjoyable, even when you're not in bed.

Pillars of cloud drifted into the corridor. Wisps and strands, till the noise in the hall vanished entirely.

An angel with four wings flew in and was hovering high in the hallway as a ray of light went up into the sky. He was surrounded by starlight, which appeared to the bystanders like a glowing thing.

Another one soared in just as this one was steadiing.

They encircled the hall's upper area one after the other in elegant stances. With their silver robes swinging in the mist, they carried harps, and their lovely, ordered flapping wings evoked the sound of paradise birds taking flight from Erian Island.

Starlight fragments littered the floor in front of the hall.

Just then, a pale gold figure darted past the stunned onlookers, leaping up and dancing like a shooting star before coming to a halt in the middle of the angelic group. A face as dazzling as the moon was revealed by the wind that lifted Raphael's golden hair. He closed his eyes gently, looked at the hall's middle pool, and joined his hands in prayer. Occasionally, one of his massive golden six wings would drop a dazzling feather.

With their fingertips resting on the harp strings, the angels encircling them also closed their eyes.

Angels' faces eventually became blurry in the music as countless flowers and stars dropped from the strings.

Raphael sang the incantation aloud while being watched by innumerable angels: "From the tender caress of a gentle breeze, to the wild rampage of a tornado; From the gentle rustling on treetops at dawn, to the mournful cries under the illusory moon at midnight."

stepping over the edge of dreams and entering reality;

Sketching the start of grief and continuing to the very conclusion."

Simultaneously, the bottom of the pool was being moved by something restless that resembled a python that was on the verge of consuming everything. More akin to a Pandora's box ready to release an unlimited supply of evils.

"Illusory lord of the final days, lend me your supreme power, shatter the chaos of hope!" Raphael exclaimed as his eyes opened, gleaming hollow.

A loud bang emerged from the water at the same moment, resembling thunderclaps falling from the sky!

Like the rushing waves, the turbulent colorful boat, the furious fire serpent, or a white dragon venturing into the sea! Water splattering repeatedly, breaking into waves, boiling, rushing, and overpowering!

Hail flew everywhere as snow-laden thunderstorms spiraled down from the sky!

As if they intended to rip apart the silent emptiness and draw out the new blood of the ink night, snowflakes and violent winds entwined and rotated in their race skyward!

Raphael extended his hands and slowly raised them, palms up.

Glass shards bounced across the earth, and the whole castle shook.

Like a river roaring through a canyon! The fierce wind made the horses gallop!

A massive tree tore through the earth, bursting through every obstacle and shooting straight up into the blue sky!

The blackness was highlighted by the vivid green leaves.

Trenches of vines entwined in the water, tree roots like hard talons, spreading downward, gripping the earth tightly. A vibrant light flashed at the same moment.

I squinted as best I could.

Raphael plummeted from the sky like an arrow to a swan. The person nearest to him, Metatron, stood motionless as others raced forward to get hold of him. Gently pointing to the tree, Raphael said, "I've revived it."

"So what?" With cold gaze, Metatron stood far from the tree, surrounded by angels.

I had never seen him appear that callous before.

With a weary grin, Raphael said, "Happy birthday, Metatron, Your Highness."

The angels started to sing as Galingvaja's wind blew across them.

With its luscious branches resembling the Titan gods shown in old Byzantine artworks, the enormous tree stood solidly in the middle of the hall, reaching the heavens and treading on the ground.

With a swift emotional adjustment, Metatron knelt down to give Raphael a shoulder pat and said, "Thank you for your gift, I will cherish it."

Raphael, who was obviously grateful, closed his eyes, looking as though he had run out of energy.

"That is the Tree of Life." I think Azael noticed my blank expression as he spoke helplessly, "Judah is the city with the greatest historical legends out of the seven heavens. Prince Metatron is the owner of the Garden of Righteousness, which includes both this city and the Eden outside. The Tree of Life was the emblem of the Garden of Righteousness until it was taken down. It's a good day; the Tree of Life has come back to life. Lost souls can be rescued and lower angels can reclaim their revelations in the future."

"Was it Prince Raphael who destroyed the Tree of Life?"

Azael's lips tightened, "I'm not sure. Ask Prince Lucifer, please."

I shook my head reflexively, looking at Lucifer by the window and saying, "I'm not curious."

"You are curious, but you don't dare to admit it."

I became motionless.

"His Highness has seen even more," declared Azael, spreading his hands. "I've seen many like you." Do you believe anyone can be tricked by your tiny tricks? However, we all ignore it."

"Someone like me?"

As he got closer, Azaelsquinted his eyes and moved his mouth but not his face. "Today, pretending to be struck by lightning, lying still at the door, kissing Prince Metatron, giving strange gifts... it's all a deliberate ploy, isn't it?"

Smack!

I struck Azael's nose with a hook punch, causing him to conceal it. He then wiped away the blood and looked at me in shock.

"If you talk to me with that kind of lecherous attitude towards women again, I'll beat you to a pulp!" I said, adjusting Lucifer's huge coat.

Azael was taken aback even further.

After observing the display from the sidelines, Samael also rushed over and gave me a thorough examination, saying, "God, he really isn't an ordinary fool..."

I tried to punch Samael horizontally, but he grabbed it.

"Hey, why are you striking me when I'm just telling the truth? And why do you act in such an impolite manner? Could you perhaps be more polite?"

"Samael." "You guys go first, I have something to discuss with him," Lucifer waved as he approached them.

He gave me another wine glass. I accepted it but refrained from drinking, feeling a little uncomfortable as I watched the two of them go. Moreover, Lucifer only shook his wine glass, his eyes the colour of the ocean.Raphael was escorted out by Metatron."

I took a silent sip of the wine because I became really anxious when I was alone with Lucifer.

"I didn't expect you to have quite the alcohol tolerance," Lucifer said as he brought me to the window. This type of wine is best consumed slowly by most people."

"Does my alcohol tolerance need to be mentioned? I wouldn't mind having another glass!"

I poured myself another glass, thinking I would wait to sip it. But then I noticed Lucifer grinning at me, and for some reason I took another sip. This wine really made you feel inebriated fast. After I finished this glass, I quickly started to feel a little lightheaded. Unable to contain myself any longer, I leaned against the window and questioned, "Your Highness, do you believe that people can travel through time?"

"Of course, there is a door of time in the heavenly realm."

"Is it true?" With a hiccup, I turned to face Lucifer and said, "Then, Your Highness, can you help me enter the door of time?"

"I can assist you, but first you must determine if you are dreaming or not. I might transport you into a dream of a different era if you're already dreaming.

You won't be in control of yourself at that moment."

"How can this be a dream since I can feel things now? Furthermore, wouldn't you also be a fraudulent person if this were a dream?

Lucifer said with a little smirk, "What is real? What is untrue? It doesn't matter if this is my reality—it might still be your dream.

I shook my head, unable to comprehend, adding, "Then I'll never be able to know."

"Actually, knowing too clearly is meaningless." "I know a child who grew up carefree under the love of his parents," he said, lowering his eyes, long lashes, and a smile still playing at the corner of his lips. But he lost his smile permanently since he discovered something he hated knowing."

" "What was that?"

"He was merely a piece of trash; the people he loved disregarded the real him. Regardless of his accomplishments and exceptional qualities, he lacked a whole soul."

I was unable to fully comprehend Lucifer's intentions.

But anyone would find it intolerable to be in such a predicament.

"So where is he now?"

"I don't know either."

I had eyes I couldn't believe. There seems to be a hint of grief in Lucifer. However, he grinned as usual and asked, "Why would you want to go somewhere else? Which is worse, being unhappy in the here and now or being unhappy in the celestial realm?"

Lucifer peered out the window, his blue eyes slightly marred by the white crescent moon. Jerusalem City, with its historic architecture and pointy tower tops, appeared as a hook beneath the crescent moon. It was shrouded in clouds and constant mist, appearing as illusive as a dream.

The mother of a West Virginia Black Bear shifter sobbed, "Thank you," wrapping her arms tightly around Miguel and Javier. "I'm so grateful that you saved my baby!" The guy who was her husband was crouched down behind her, his arms encircling little Emily, and he had just as many tears in his eyes as his wife had.

Miguel advised her to take good care of her. "She is not worthy of going through that again."

The mother swore, "Never." "I promise never to let her leave my sight."

Before her parents led her to their car and drove away in the direction of home, Emily arrived to give Javier and Miguel one last hug.

As he watched the dust fly, Javier sighed and said, "Well, that was the last of them." Now that everyone is secure with their parents,

Miguel brought Javier in close enough to give him a head kiss with his arm around him. "We made a wise decision," he remarked, as though Javier required confirmation. "And now is the perfect moment for us to take care of ourselves."

"Oh?" Javier enquired, piqued. He trailed Miguel through the front door and into the kitchen, where he began removing cookware from a cabinet. "Such as what?"

Miguel chuckled, "Like eat something besides chicken fingers and macaroni and cheese." He took out a bottle of tequila from the freezer and then a large piece of meat from the refrigerator.

"So, what is your preference for steak?"

Javier had not had a drink in what seemed like an eternity, and the tequila hit him square in the skull. Still, he enjoyed the sense of reduced inhibitions. Oh my goodness, he adored the steak.

He gushed, "This is fantastic," as he took bites of the perfectly cooked meat. Miguel was correct; it had been weeks since they had eaten anything resembling chicken nuggets and macaroni and cheese, and his body was desperately missing the protein found in steak.

The two men had laughed and discussed almost everything at the supper that they had been unable to discuss with the kids. They shared their experiences coming out, as well as the friends that stood by them and the ones who broke up with them. They discussed their life journeys, starting points, and current locations. They chatted for a while until the sun had long since set and they were almost out of tequila.

"I guess Miami is the place for you then?" Miguel inquired. He observed the smile gradually go from Javier's face as he persisted in paying more attention to the shot glass than Miguel.

Leaning his back on the chair, he finally said, "I don't know what the place is for me anymore." "I believe—I believe that all of the crime is beginning to affect me." That encounter with the twelve girls was fortunate. It was a blessing that they were all still alive and could be with their families. However, things almost never finish like that. I have held the dead in my arms who were just minutes from death."

Miguel stood up, leaned across the table, and took Javier's chair by the seat. He dragged it all the way towards him with his powerful hands, allowing Javier to rest his head on his shoulder. He smiled for a moment at the gesture, and Miguel felt a twinge of satisfaction at his display of joy.

Miguel enquired, "What were they all running from?"

Sighing, Javier shrugged his shoulders. He had had enough of talking about it. Rather, he desired to snuggle deeper into Miguel's chest and spend years sleeping there. Perhaps waken occasionally for sex, but that was all.

"Very different things. A few of them became involved with the drug cartel in that area. acted on their animal instincts rather than giving in to their human desire. Some were evading capture after being discovered by human poachers. Numerous factors existed, but none of them appeared to be worth dying for. Not with me.

Miguel gave Javier a tender kiss on the top of his head and tightened his embrace around him. Miguel moved his lips down the side of Javier's face and said, "Sounds like you need a break."

As Javier closed his eyes, a tiny groan leaked out of his throat. "I do," he squealed. He reached up and put his fingers around the big, strong forearms of the man who was holding him. He could sense the warmth beneath his skin, the blood, the tendons, and the muscle, all of which were flawlessly coordinating to keep him near the man who had saved his life.

"How come you feel so wonderful?" Javier cocked his head back to inquire.

Miguel harrumphed, his lips edging closer to Javier's, "Because." "It was meant to be me and you."

His lips fell over Javier's in the most delicious way, and the two men melted into one another, allowing their passion to override their physical differences. With his legs wide out to allow his lover's hand to easily pull down the zipper and undo the button on his trousers, Javier slid onto Miguel's lap right away. When Miguel did exactly that and he discovered his palm wrapped around the thickness of his cock, he gasped and broke their kiss.

He brought his cock to a painfully hard point with a long, sensual stroke of his fingers. Miguel used his other hand to go inside Javier's shirt and reach his well-defined chest, where he persistently adjusted and tormented his turgid nipples. Everything faded away as Javier caved in to the seductive taunts of the alpha shifter, including his anxieties and doubts about the future of his existence.

"Shall we get you in bed now?" Miguel enquired in a low, seductive voice. Javier gave a swift nod in agreement, and he felt his body being raised and taken inside Miguel's bedroom right away. It made sense now why he had never been brought to bed before. The gesture seemed very personal, like it was only meant for lovers to exchange, not casual flings from the gay bar down the street.

Miguel started taking off his clothes in the bedroom, and Javier soon joined him, kicking off his trousers and tugging at his shirt as if he couldn't get the clothes off of him quickly enough. When they were both completely nude, Javier thanked the gods above for giving him such a strong, attractive guy, even if it was just for a short time, and gazed up at Miguel in all his magnificence. His gaze swept slowly over his nude body, registering each muscle group, vein, and, at last, his sex. The sex between his thick, long, well-defined legs, which stood at attention for him. He begged

Miguel to let him taste it since it made his mouth water.

Miguel gave Javier a sly chuckle as he held the back of his head and led him towards his goal. Though he had to pry open Javier's mouth wider than it had ever been, he pushed himself in. He occupied all of his partner's space, but none of them complained. Javier meekly sat at the edge of the bed for several minutes, sucking Miguel's cock as though it were his sole job for the rest of his life.

While he was doing this, Miguel spoke to him in hushed, comforting whispers. Javier had strange muscular tremors and spasms due to the velvety quality of his voice. It immediately made him question if he would be able to fulfil his deepest desire that evening.

Miguel drew him away just far enough to meet his gaze, as though he could read his thoughts. They both wanted more, and there was nothing that could stop them from getting it. After extracting his cock entirely from Javier's mouth, Miguel started massaging his partner's jaw. He was always aware of his size and the potential for great suffering in the event that they weren't properly cared for.

Javier said, "More, please. I want more." The intercourse was going to sting a little, he could tell just by looking at him, but he was craving it. He yearned for the sensation of possessing such a powerful man within himself.

"Switch around," Miguel gave the order. Without delay, Javier made his way to the wrought iron headboard in order to have something solid to hold onto. Miguel's fingers, dripping with warm lubricant, widened his cheeks and sank deep inside of him as his fingers were weaving through the metal design.

The ecstasy of the invasion made his eyes roll to the back of his head. He felt as though he could spread his legs wide and buckle his knees when he was touched in just the right way. He practically begged Miguel to go on when he asked if he wanted more.

Miguel complied without hesitation and quickly pushed his way inside Javier's personal area. He moved very slowly at first—almost excruciatingly so. Javier then started to move quicker and harder as his groans grew louder and more frequent. He thrust himself within, filled with a fresh enthusiasm for life and pleasure. The intensity of it all caused Javier's cock to jerk and spill cecum all over the bed, which he watched with passionate ecstasy.

That's it, Miguel exclaimed, feeling a surge of exhilaration. "Come get me, give me a spill."

Miguel hurriedly followed Javier, who was wallowing in the bed and groaning the name of his lover.

"Why does Pandora seem to have bars in every other building?"

"What are your expectations? The best course of action in a situation like this is to drown your sorrows. Business is growing there.

That makes sense, I guess. I'm curious how these bars all manage to remain in operation. There is intense rivalry amongst people.

"Perhaps so many people exist who are only seeking intoxication."

Andrea gave me a raised eyebrow. She was by definition a Beta. She did, however, occasionally exhibit the astute mind of an Alpha.

“All right,” I nodded. "There are a lot of people in need here."

"You're only realising that now?"

Not at all. But I'm having problems understanding everything. I'm not entitled to toss away my money just because I'm wealthy. To try to contribute to this aspect of Dirge, I still need to figure out how to invest my money.

She questioned, "And that's why you invited me to come along?" "Because you want my assistance in deciding how to allocate your funds?"

"Bingo."

As we walked down the sidewalk, I gave her a wink.

In Pandora, the day appeared to be typical. Since I hadn't spent much time here, I could only presume that everyone lived in poverty. When you realised that the worst thing about the terrible poverty surrounding me was the view, it wasn't as unpleasant. Even though they were so depressed, the people themselves appeared to be going about their lives and making ends meet.

"I'm not sure where to start," I murmured.

She suggested, "Maybe you should invest in a pub itself." It would be profitable. Someone with your level of skill could eliminate your rivals.

I get what you're saying. They would then have no choice but to start another business. Rather than selling booze, they would need to pick up a skill. tailors. Woodworking. A rising sector in Dirge is the agricultural industries.

"It looks like a promising opportunity."

"Even so... All of these pubs seem to have something in common that keeps them in business. It's not just the alcohol, either.

"And just what is it?"

I came to a halt. I pivoted to face the bar directly across from us. The location was unremarkable. There was no signage, and the windows were filthy. Just outside of it, men were observing me closely. Their odours were overpowered by the overpowering stench of alcohol on them.

"Why don't we identify it precisely?" I told her.

"Your ideas are really quite radical."

She was unable to reject me. Andrea knew me well enough to know that I enjoyed taking chances. I didn't act as though I owned every location I entered because of my wealth. I was the alpha. I have to let people know that.

We entered the bar, and I could feel the eyes on me from everyone around us. The majority of them were alphas by nature. A few of Omegas aimlessly roamed the area. For the most part, they were taking care of the lonely Alphas and going about their own business.

When they saw me with Andrea, I could only guess what was going through their minds. An Alpha Jaguar and her female buddy, a Beta. I was certain that they had never seen a couple like us before, even without my costume, which was enough to make for an odd sight.

When I approached the bar, the barman approached me with reluctance.

"What are you looking for?" he mocked me.

"Just a few beverages," I said. "Please give me your best."

"My best, eh? All I have is inexpensive beer.

"Yes, cheap beer," I replied with a warm grin.

The barman narrowed his eyes at me and gave me a hard look. I dug inside my pocket and took out a piece of gold while he poured me and Andrea a glass of beer. I placed it on the countertop. With a swift motion, the barman picked it up and began to inspect it.

Andrea remarked, "I'm assuming you don't get much gold in here very often."

To which the barman said, "Look around." "Do you believe that any of these people are wearing gold? If I was lucky, I might get a few copper pieces.

I looked around the throng. They were all rugged, tough males, I noticed. They had boots on their feet and tight, stained denim on. They looked like they belonged to a gang since they had leather vests with similar patches.

As we savoured our beer, Andrea stood behind me. She grimaced at the filthy mugs and her face became even more unpleasant when she took a sip.

She remarked, "I spend too much time with you." "I'm ruined from all that red wine."

"Now, now," I murmured. "I should look into helping these people, you were the one who suggested." It would be inappropriate to offend one of their few pleasures in life.

As I sipped my nasty drink, I kept scanning the bar. Everybody in the pub was equally resentful.

"They dress in an interesting way," I remarked, surveying the gathering.

"Cyclists on motorcycles," Andrea answered.

"What?" I asked, looking in her direction.

"Cyclist groups," she clarified. "To show which club they belong to, they wear patches. It's a more blatant method of expressing their loyalty.

"I observe... It is possible to extract the beast from the pack, but not the other way around.

"The pack mentality is still present in them even though they no longer reside in the woods. All of them have the opportunity to stay in the comfort of a group thanks to motorbike clubs. It offers them the highest odds of surviving.

It was expected that some would prefer to continue living in packs despite having access to all of man's comforts.

That, I believe, is it.

"What is it?" Andrea answered.

That's why establishments like this provide these clubs and packs. It is their location. That's how these bars are able to continue operating. Here, every club is just a pack that has delineated its area.

Are you implying that a location like Pandora has no chance of success? that things would always be as they are?"

"Not indefinitely. All I'm stating is that some people will decide not to alter their behaviour. And this is how they continue the ancient customs."

"Hi!"

A voice cut across my friendly exchange with Andrea. The man who was suddenly standing next to me turned to face us both.

His skin was tan, and he had a shaven head. His pupils were hardly visible, and his eyes were white.

Although he was large, he didn't seem to loom over me. His abs and chest muscles were blatantly visible behind the leather vest he was wearing. His skin was covered in ink, suggesting that he has likely faced someone with a similar brazen demeanour before.

coffee. I was awakened by the delicious aroma and found myself drooling. I could feel the heat fog lifting miraculously from my head, and my appetite was raging. However, I was by myself and his arms were not around me. Eager to see Brad, I clambered out from under the covers and tugged at the tent flap.

My muscles tensed up in relief that he was there. I rushed towards him, my thighs sticky with dried slick, my cock immediately hardening again at the sight of him watching over the camp stove, feeling my skin break out in goosebumps in the chilly air. Then he was looking up at me, the serious contemplation on his face fragmenting into — what? Was it affection? Is that possible? — In any case, I wanted to believe it was love, and the happiness nearly split my heart. I was too glad to speak, and at the very least, I could tell he was happy to see me.

However, he comprehended. In bed as well as out, he seemed to know precisely what I needed. I was quite fortunate.

"A moment, please." He moved into the tent after taking a few steps. After assisting me with putting on my tee and trousers, he pulled a sweater over my head. "Now that I'm kissing you, you won't freeze."

His expression shifted. "What's going on?"

He could tell that tears had welled up in my eyes.

Nothing. I'm just overjoyed. I'm so happy you're taking care of me.

His expression cleared. "I'm relieved about that." He drew me in closer. "It's lunchtime, but let's have a proper good morning nonetheless." And his mouth struck mine, robbing, insisting. My legs seemed to dissolve as I opened out to him. I'm glad he's supporting me because otherwise I would be dripping around his feet.

He was also tough. My pulse rate increased to race mode as soon as I felt him pressing against my cock through our clothes. I could feel his laugh while we were kissing, and I started to tug him in the direction of the tent.

Oh no. I have to feed you some food first. Brad reluctantly seemed to move his mouth away from mine. "I have to take care of you."

I nodded as the warmth from that remark filled me from head to toe and I smelled the food warming beneath the coffee scent. Brad stirred the pan and offered me a drink.

"I fear MREs. Then I realised we could change course and temporarily abandon ship here. His eyes ascended the mountain. "A few days of hiding away would be nice for us."

I could feel the nervousness in his voice. "What is the issue?"

He grinned as he turned to face me. "Man and wolf, I want to learn more about you. There is nothing wrong with that.

I gave a headshake. "That would be nice. But there's something on your mind. I'm not too weak to give it to you.

He appeared stunned. "No, no. Ryan, I didn't mean that at all. He fell to the ground and took a seat next to me. "Please trust me—we're safe here." My shoulders were tightly encircled by his arm. "However, I have informed the federal authorities about Fox and the reopening of the Academy."

My chest constricted with panic, and I tried not to show it. He squeezed me very lightly.

It's alright. Nothing or no one will be able to harm you. I refuse to do so. He smiled a little. "Up in those mountains, no one will find us."

He made contact with my hand. "Suck in your coffee. Soon the food will be ready, and then we may explore. He made a grab at his own cup. "I'll probably have to go help clean up the mess when we get to Blakestown, but I'll make sure you're safe with Jude and Aiden."

He must have smiled at my perplexed expression.

"Until Aiden ran away from the Academy, Jude was a friend of mine back home. They recently had a baby, and you would still be there if we hadn't learned about the Academy from him.

"Or sold." I shuddered.

However, you're not. You're safe because you're with me. We're secure. collectively. He spoke in a very forceful tone. "How about we have lunch?"

I was taken aback by how hungry I was, and Brad grinned as he passed over his mostly consumed food. I swallowed it down after giving it some thought because I was so hungry. Another cookie packet went down quite nicely, and I watched, stuffed, as Brad cleaned and tidied the camp. He was folding and putting things away in designated spots, and it made me think of his time in the military. He let me assist a little, but I restrained him well enough that I had to sit on a tree stump and wait. He turned off his phone and concealed it under a blanket pack, which I witnessed, and then he locked the truck and approached me, extending his hand.

"Leave now." He had a raspy voice. "I want you to see yourself as a wolf and become my pack mate."

I grasped his hand as he navigated the forest, gaining some distance from the truck. Brad circled around, observing everything with a wolfish fascination. I watched him run towards a tree, jump up onto a branch, and then drop back to the ground, hiding the truck key.

After passing a few clearings, he came to a halt and smiled at me. "All right, let's hang our clothing here. They are no longer necessary.

My cock sprang with yearning. My heat was over, why was I so aroused at the thought of getting naked? I turned away slightly, knowing I was blushing and my gut clenched at the sound of his throaty chuckle. Then his arms were around me and his face was nuzzling into my shirt.

"We've plenty of time for that, this trip." His infectious excitement was catching and we hurriedly stowed our clothes in the hollow of a tree branch.

"Okay, let's shift and go running." His eyes were bright with passion as he watched me and I watched him too. My mate was a huge gray wolf, his powerful haunches and deep chest a true measure of the man he was too. I knew my stringy leanness wasn't a match for him, but he came to me and laid his head over my shoulders for a moment. Then he was nudging me upwards, and with a bound he was away, racing through the trees in an ecstasy of joy. I matched him stride for stride, a feeling of joy and freedom and belonging filling me.

Before heading out to supper, Tim and Jonathan stopped for drinks at the pack house. The pack house was stunning and quite large. It also had views of the sea, a swimming area, vegetable and flower gardens, and an abundance of space for shifters to run for recreation, sport, and mating rites. Having formally asked to join the Timber Ridge Pack, Jonathan felt it would be wise to get to know as many other pack members as he could in the hopes of making some new ones. For the first time in his life, he wouldn't have to justify his social life to his family.

"Jon, do you still recall our Alpha Pack Master, Nash?" The men exchanged handshakes. "Alpha Nash, it's good to see you again. I'm excited for tonight's dinner." More significantly, though, I am incredibly appreciative of your invitation to become a member of the Timber Ridge Pack. stated Jonathan. "We can always use more young alphas, but the pack benefits the most since you agreed to practice medicine on pack lands and serve as our chief medical officer," the alpha pack master grinned. The three packs have required a full-time medical professional ever since the Eastern Shore Shifters Pack split up. Additionally, there are a lot of young omegas here who Arron will definitely expose you to. Permit me to introduce you to my friend Arron. Jonathan Rayse is the newest member of our pack, Arron. Arron is a fantastic cook and stands by my side as Alpha Mate, providing important assistance to our pack members. With a flush, Arron held out his hand, surprising and delighting Jonathan as he reached out and gave the Alpha Mate a hearty shake.

It's a pleasure to meet you, Aaron. I'm excited to find out more about the pack and how I can support its operations. stated Jonathan. "Well, we can talk about the pack in greater detail during supper later tonight. In fact, we are organizing a formal pack meeting for this Friday, which is the next full moon. During dinner, Nash will introduce you to the entire pack. If you'd like, you can run with the pack under the full moon. Arron answered. "I think I'll join the run." Jonathan murmured, as Tim wave from the other side of the spacious living room. "Pardon me, I believe I am going to meet some additional pack members."

"Jon, let me introduce you to Alec Gregg before we head out to dinner." Alec extended his hand to shake Jonathan's, and Jonathan could tell that Alec was a beta based on the way he held the hand. "And this is Chase, his friend." Jonathan went to shake hands with Chase, but he gave him an embrace instead. He mentally jotted down a note to ask Tim about the gesture later. "Alec is the head of security and Nash's second beta, answering only to me." Tim introduced Alec to Jonathan and then smiled mischievously at him.

We just laid there for a bit till Ed eventually slipped out of my ass and I looked over to find him grinning at me. He said, "That really was something," and I couldn't help but nod in agreement.

Yes, it truly was, I answered, leaning in to give him a kiss without saying anything more.

I became a top for the first time a short while afterward. Anal intercourse was fantastic; in fact, I think I preferred topping Ed to bottoming him, but it was still insignificant in comparison to my enjoyment of blowing a guy away.

I had butt sex with five people over the course of the next several months, but the most sex I had was with two of them, Ed and Sam.

With summer fast approaching, I started to feel like I was an authority in blow jobs, great, hard anal sex, and all those sexy man-on-man actives.

But the thing about summer coming was that there was one thing I was not prepared for, and it was the thing I was most looking forward to. I would be in my hometown instead of the town where I attend college. This meant that going out and getting some hot gay fun wasn't safe for ten long weeks. The week before we celebrated our school's out, I made an effort to boost my libido before I went by going out on the town with five guys I knew. I even got double teamed during that crazy trip, with one guy beating my ass while his boyfriend penetrated my face.

Ultimately, I returned home exhausted but joyful, feeling like I would be fine for the summer despite having a painful ass.

However, I was losing my mind by the start of July. I started dreaming about doing blow jobs because I was so desperate for cock.

No, the word "wanted" was incorrect. I was in need of cock.

That summer, my closest friend Greg arrived home later than usual—in fact, he didn't show up until July 3. I'd always been close to Greg, and together we were quite the team in high school. All the females adored Greg because he was so attractive. Greg adored the girls back.

Naturally, I hadn't told him that I was gay because, let's face it, there was a foolish part of me that always wanted Greg. He was far too attached to women.

That is, I believed.

The two of us were at his parents' house on July 9. We had all been hanging around and catching up since a few of our common friends had dropped over earlier in the evening. It was quite the celebration at first, especially since his parents weren't in town. But as the evening went on, our companions started to disappear, leaving just the two of us.

Greg had seemed a touch weird all night. Needless to say, I wasn't thrilled about it. We were feeling pretty good after working through a bunch of Jameson whiskey and breaking into his dad's liquor cupboard. Nevertheless, I had known Greg for a very long time, and I thought he was a little... "off." I was unable to pinpoint the exact cause of it, so I reasoned that perhaps I was just going crazy.

He turned to face me and said something as we sat on his porch, gazing out over the remainder of the quaint town we had both grown up in. It was not even midnight.

I have to tell you something, dude. I'm saying... I have a message for you. I believe. I'm saying... I'm concerned that you might go crazy, because I simply... calm down, dude? Alright, Owen? You cool as you chill?

I gave a nod. I turned my head away from him and gazed at the drowsy lights below. Avoiding immediate eye contact seemed to be beneficial. Furthermore, had I continued to gaze into those tender blue eyes, I might have become so enthralled that I could not resist the need to lean in and give him a kiss. That would have been really uncomfortable.

"So, dude, what's this thing you have to tell me?" I asked, sipping from my glass of red tail.

He cleared his throat with a gulp of beer after swallowing hard, "I think," and then resumed. "I believe that in high school, I might have been lying to myself. telling you lies. To all of you.

I glanced back at him out of curiosity. His fucking eyes were just so damned attractive.

"What's up with that?"

He declared, "I think I like dudes."

It appeared as though he had just shot me in the abdomen. My entire body began to tremble, and I was at a loss for how to stop myself. that was unbelievable to me that he had said that. Greg, are you gay? It was not conceivable in any manner. There was simply no way. Though, to be honest, I had fantasized that he was into guys.

"What leads you to believe that? In high school, you were the epitome of cool. The ideal man for ladies.

He gave a shrug. I understand, but I believe that my lack of genuine concern had a role. However, I got pretty wasted over spring break and... I got duped by a dude in the end. Additionally, I enjoyed it. A colossal amount. Much more than any other time a girl has done it. Additionally... In the end, I gave the favor back. That was also enjoyable to me.

I forcefully gulped. My heart was pounding. It was unbelievable to me. My penis quivered. In my whole life, I wanted Greg more than I wanted anyone or anything else.

"Did you repeat it?"

He nodded after beginning to shake his head. "There's this college student who is openly gay, complete with a lisp. He's ridiculed by all, but he seems content and has lots of attractive girlfriends. At a party late one night, I made a move on him. He blew me while leading me into the restroom. told me that more guys than I would have thought hit him up. That is all, though.

"Are you drunk at that moment?"

Greg gave a headshake. Not at all. The problem is, I find it unable to shake that picture. A sexy man is blowing my mind. God, I guess I'm homosexual as hell.

I answered, "Well, there's only one way to find out," got to my feet, turned around, and knelt down in front of him. I took off his pants and grasped his cock without saying anything more. My best friend had a good thick one, and I had seen it in the locker rooms previously.

He was already halfway hard, which surprised and delighted me.

"Dude," mumbled he.

"Shh," I whispered, removing it from his shorts and stroking it till he woke up completely.

"Why not just let something happen that you've wanted?" I mentioned.

After a moment of staring into my eyes, Greg nodded. Like me, he knew when to shut up.

For a time, I licked and sucked on his cock, savoring the delicious, muddy taste and aroma as it slid between my lips. At that moment, I had everything I could possibly need or want. There, with him between my lips, was all I needed. Greg repeated just how I wanted him to, so I sucked and slurped. He was ideal for it and ecstatic to have received the wonderful release he had been longing for and required.

That was, I believe, the moment when both of our aspirations were realized, and that made me happy.

"Whoa, you're really good at that," stumbled Greg. I just gurgled and coughed as I emptied my throat on his cock, not replying. He grasped the back of my head and began to thrust up, unable to control himself. I suppose it was understandable that he wanted to screw me in the face. It's difficult, but I don't mind at all, and it's really simple to lose yourself in the here and now.

When his penis began to twitch, I knew he was getting near. I just relaxed my throat and let him keep fucking it; that was my only response. He stumbled, "Shit!" and then I felt his creamy seed explode in my throat.

I continued slurping and sucking as I effortlessly ingested it all.

I let go of his cock and stared up at him with a nasty smile on my face after a minute, or until I was certain he was clean.

"How did you find that to be?" I enquired.

"Absolutely amazing. I had no idea that you had done this previously.

With a nod, I got up and guided him inside while keeping an eye on his hand.

"Well, it was only this fall, but this definitely wasn't my first time."

"Well, dude, I don't know about this; we are best friends."

I kissed him silently. When he kissed me back with the same intensity that I felt, I was ecstatic.

I pulled back and placed my hands on his chest after we had a kiss that lasted only a few seconds but seemed like an eternity. "Calm down, man. It's going to be enjoyable. If you enjoy getting head as much as you enjoy sucking cock, that is.

After I drifted off, Greg gave me another kiss and ushered me into the bedroom. Greg licked his lips as we both undressed silently. He must have enjoyed what he saw. In actuality, every other man I had dated had informed me that I had a good cock. I was thick, uncut, and lengthy. Alternatively, I was a free-range, homegrown kind of man, as the locals would say.

She knew enough to be scared when she saw him for the first time. Despite the man's human appearance, Saniyah recognized him as one of the Dragon Overlords. Nevertheless, there was something about him that didn't fit the tales she had grown up hearing.

Saniyah would have anticipated the Dragonborn to have immediately torn her limb from limb, given the legends that were passed down through the generations of Angeliym. Their people's war had been as brutal and cruel as it had been. The conflict only came to an end when the Angeliym managed to flee underground and a shaky peace was established, according to which the Dragonborn would dominate the surface of the earth and the Angeliym would be allowed to exist beneath it.

However, Drakka, the crown prince, who stood in front of her, wasn't at all what she had anticipated. tall, broad in the shoulders, and powerful. His dark, long hair reached his midback, and his deep, black eyes had the appearance of being both soulful and bottomless.

Saniyah was captivated to him right away because of his attractive appearance. She pondered absently whether the ability to compel others was one of the Dragonborn's many abilities.

With a scared whimper, the youngster behind her adjusted his feet and clutched to her gown. With a slight smile, Saniyah returned his gaze with her own.

"Everything will work out," she muttered.

With fear in his eyes, he widened them and remained silent. Saniyah pivoted to observe the guard of the prince riding off. After they had vanished, he turned to face her and gave her a kind grin while twirling his blade around in his fingers and putting it back into its sheath.

"All right," he murmured. "Should we have a conversation?"

Saniyah remarked, "I don't think we have anything to talk about."

The man pointed to the youngster who was hiding behind her and said, "I disagree." "To begin with, the boy."

"I'll stop you from hurting him."

Drakka grinned. "I wish not to cause him harm."

"So, what are you wanting?"

He gave her a gentle grin as he glanced at her. "I hope that all of this taught him a lesson," he remarked. "And never again stole anything."

Saniyah spun around and sent a scared look into the wide eyes of the youngster who returned her gaze. He whispered, "I

With a shake of her head, she tried to banish the images from her mind. She focused on a point just beyond him as the fire between her thighs burned out of control. She briefly wondered why she had such vivid thoughts about a man she just met. She cleared her throat and tried to focus on the present – specifically, the danger of the present.

"So what now?" she asked. "What about us? Are you going to haul me away? Kill me where I stand?"

The Dragonborn prince looked at her and then looked away – almost like he was a shy, awkward boy or something. Saniyah found it endearing – and then remembered that he was dangerous. A mortal enemy of her people. At least, she was trying to make herself believe that.

"Actually, I thought that maybe we could walk together for a while," he said. "Have a conversation."

"No!" Someone wept and was silent.

I lowered my head. Agnarr pulled out his sword and gave it to the Dragon King, hilt first.

"I promise to serve my people with all of my loyalty. My sword is yours, along with whatever else you may require. Do you promise to protect me in return?

With the sword in his hand, the Dragon King placed the blade against my brother's shoulder.

"I promise to keep you and your people safe. Accept Astrid, Yngvild's daughter, as a testament to your sincerity. To make sure Astrid is safe, I'll take your brother.

"Erlendr?" flinchedAgnarr.

With a harsh tone, the king said, "You swore your loyalty."

I closed my eyes to the outside world and whispered, "I will go, your majesty. I will go, brother."

"A deal has been reached." Taking the sword, the Dragon King cut his palm.

Red blood trickled down the blade.

He gave Agnarr back the bloodied sword. Not as deeply as the King, Agnarr cut himself on the opposite side. After sheathing it, he got up.

"Yngvild, divide our army," the Dragon King commanded. He surveyed us with his eyes and said, "Leave them with enough to cover and start building defences," along with food.

Bid farewell to Astrid. "We have to march back to Mount Sorrow and bid farewell to your brother," King Kolbeinn said to Yngvild. "You are coming with us now," he said to me.

I shuddered at something about the way his eyes scanned my form. For a brief while, I lost my courage. I peered at the settlement.

But my house, I remarked.

Agnarr growled, "Be thankful you did not die this night." "Brother, take care of yourself," he said, clasping my hand. Until our next meeting.

I told her, "Take good care of your little one. I hope to see her grow into a strong, tall woman."

He gave my arm a shake. My hand had a small amount of blood on it as he withdrew.

"Enter now!" Yngvild made a call.

She yelled commands. A minimum of thirty percent of their troops split up and came back with Agnarr and Astrid. I saw my house's gates open to welcome them. I waved. Upon seeing, my archers saluted. I placed my palm on the sword's pommel and used my quiver to hook my bow onto my back. I turned my back on the only home I had ever known and followed Yngvild and the King.

Section Two

I discovered that I was overindulging in some liquid courage that I had discovered in the refrigerator. She had given me a bottle of wine one Christmas, and I had never even bothered to open it. Today, however, was a different story, and her haughty demeanour and the way she was treating me as though I were less than worthy were beginning to irritate me. I was limited in how much I could take her, but happily I was able to drown the part of me that wasn't paying attention to what she was saying.

"Sheila, please make yourself at home. I'll see you in the morning. I'm heading out for the night."

"Be still, my beating heart; my younger sister is meeting a man." You've always seemed to me like a lipstick lesbian who is eager to come out of the closet. Even though I knew she was only attempting to get under my skin, I couldn't let her. My feelings were connected to the being within me. It felt like it was just beginning to surface. That lion inside of me was getting so enraged by her presence that it wanted to rip its limbs off. As soon as you return, I want all the information. I'm positive that both I and... Once more, I drowned her out and stopped paying attention to her.

I would at most nod my head and give her a kind of noncommittal shoulder shrug. Taking a deep breath, I left, feeling as though I hadn't breathed in the four hours she had been here. Even after four hours, I still couldn't believe it, and I was itching to cut my wrists and hang myself from the tallest tree.

It was still going to be around two hours until the moon appeared. I strolled into the forest and down to the shore to observe the sun gradually setting behind the trees.

"Isn't it beautiful?" I sprang back, frightened, at the sound of a man's voice. "I simply had to pause and enjoy the view, and right now all I want to do is sit here and watch the sun set. I've already visualised it in my head because of how beautifully it reflects off the trees. He was a young man with dark hair, blue eyes, and a bulge in his jeans that would make any woman jealous. He was also 5'11" and weighed 170 pounds. He seems like he might be in his 20s to me. As I was quickly reaching the big four O, I could definitely relate to the origins of the name "cougar."

"I don't live too far away from here, and I like to do that myself." He sat there with his legs crossed, his fingers pointing out towards the lake, and his eyes closed. "I might just stop by and spend a little time with you." I took a seat and carried out his actions. It took me a while to get into this posture, but when I did, I felt as though my meditation practise had advanced significantly. Though on the inside I was seething and wanted to bash my little sister's face with my fist, I appeared cool.

"I simply appreciate the wonders that mother nature bestows upon us on a daily basis. Everybody around us takes everything for granted. All you need to do is give it some thought. At that point, you'll realise how tiny and unimportant you actually are in this universe. Though

I had never considered it in that manner before, I did notice the lake's ripples and realised they would persist long after I was gone.

I guess I could find comfort in the fact that I don't believe the shifter will live indefinitely. It would eventually give up to the might of nature or perhaps some other untamed animal that would object to it being in its domain. In a sense, I was the jungle's king—or, maybe more accurately, its queen.

"Now that I think about it, I too enjoy pausing occasionally. I allowed Mother Nature to reveal to me the reality that most people are unaware of." I could feel the hunger burning deep inside of me, and my stomach was starting to turn over.

For the first time since the animal scratched me a few years ago, I could feel the difference. Back then, I thought I was experiencing a heart attack of some kind. I never made it to a hospital at all, and before I knew it, I was waking up in a field full of deer parts.

"That people notice what I do makes me happy. I frequently believe that I am the only one who understands or even recognises the true nature of the world. My partner has a more reserved demeanour. She is gorgeous, don't get me wrong, but there seems to be a darkness within her that extends to her very being. You could say that she balances me out because I counteract her negativity with positive. He had the tone of one of those localised gurus who were always talking about the positive aspects of life, spirits, energy, and all that sort of thing. After discovering that I was a lion shifter—something I had never believed in—I started to experience what it felt like to connect with both my own and other people's emotions.

"Your girl has a bitch-like voice." He burst out laughing at those words. He went into a completely different level of frantic assault than I have ever witnessed, losing his cool and falling backwards while shrieking at the sky and trembling like a leaf.

It never occurred to me to consider it, but perhaps there was a method to eliminate this sensation of hunger. Is there a chance that I might sate the beast and give it far more control with sex? This younger man seemed like the perfect person to spend a night with. He was amazing, and even through his extremely tight t-shirt, I could see that he was made to make girls swoon at the sight of his nude body.

There was a noticeable thumping in his blue pants and he was breathing frantically when he eventually returned. I took a seat next to him and placed my hand on his knee, moving my fingers slowly till they grasped his prize.

I know it sounds completely strange, but I can't help but feel like I know that guy with the scar on his face or that we are related in some way. He and his companion leave quite soon, and I'm left with it bothering me for the remainder of the evening. I want to find out what happened.

As usual, Bobby escorts out the few customers who are still there at two and distributes the tip jar before we all leave for our homes. But I swear, there's something tense about me tonight. I leave the club feeling apprehensive. Perhaps it's the enigmatic man who looks so familiar to me, or perhaps it's the memory of the spooky man who followed me while hiding in the darkness the night before. Either way, all I want is to get home, change into some clothes that make me feel like I do, sort of, still have some dignity, and then snuggle up in bed with Stonewall at my feet.

I shiver a little bit as I stroll down the sidewalk in my mesh top and short shorts because it's an unusually cool night for Miami. The humidity has even somewhat decreased, and the sky is clear. I pause and look up into the starry sky above me. It's serene, serene, silent, and full of stars overhead; it takes me back to my early years in Connecticut. We resided in a small town with minimal light pollution and an abundance of stars, especially on stormy nights. For a brief minute, I close my eyes and am transported back to nights when Andrew and I would lie on our backs in the tree house and gaze up at the stars. I was usually the nervous one; occasionally, I would startle at the sound of an owl or the far-off sounds of vehicles travelling along the county road. Andrew would hold my hand while we fell asleep in our sleeping bags on numerous occasions when we were kids, which always gave me a sense of security and comfort.

I feel a sudden collision and a severe ache at my side before collapsing to the ground. I push open my eyes and see two males standing over me. One of them is holding a tyre iron, while the other is holding a crow bar. The person on the left is definitely the same one that was pursuing me the previous evening.

Yes, it's me, and I know you recognise me, fag. You discovered last night that I had been scheming you for a week, didn't you? It appears that he is really happy with himself.

I ought to move, that would definitely frighten them away from me. However, I'm not sure how I'll be able to change. We shifters have a basic rule that we never break: we never change in front of oblivious humans. I would most likely be banished from the clan if someone back home discovered that I had disobeyed the rule. However, I can't think of a single clan member who would genuinely want me to refrain from defending myself in some way.

We therefore want all of your money, including the huge stash you have hidden away in those tiny pockets. I might then take your ass after that. He sneers down at me, thrusts his hand, and licks his lips.

I was planning to defend myself and make a break for it, but now that I'm paralysed, all I can do is have memories to those days spent in the college locker room.

He stoops down and gives me a kick to the gut. As he yells commands at me, he gets near enough to my face that I can feel little drops of spit escaping and smell his sharp breath. "The cash?" he asks, holding out his palm flat just inches from my nose.

Grant. Daniel let out a deep moan. Stay alive!

He recoiled from the overwhelming sense of grief, attempting to keep his mind free of terror as if it were a river he may drown in.

I'm doing my hardest.

Please refrain from making jokes! Tell me what has to be done!

I must eat. Grant recommended. I believe I can recover. However, I must eat.

Daniel stopped talking and turned to leave the shelter. A riot of happy beginnings could be heard from the birds as the sky lightened to a deep mauve.

He thought with a sneer, "Really, shut the fuck up," and turned off the bird sounds. He waved his head back and forth, catching sight of a family of medium-sized hares with their pale purple ribbons.

Every painful breath Grant drew seemed to be the measure of time, and it seemed to take forever. However, it really only took a few exhausting minutes. Daniel darted across the woodland in the direction of the hare family, catching them off guard as two of them peered excitedly from their burrow to nibble in the mist of early dawn. With a ferocity that took him by surprise, he dove headfirst into their hollow and with one clean snap of his jaws, snatched two.

He hurried back to the cave, the hares still wriggling in his jaws, calling out to Grant to hang on across the soul-space. He wriggled back into the depression and, with a hopeful nosy towards Grant's mouth, placed the hot, limp carcasses beneath his muzzle.

Grant, hurry up. Here, he said in an upbeat manner.

Grant appeared to be drifting off to sleep for a brief while, but he quickly opened his jaws and licked the blood from the nearest hare's open throat. The pulsating life force wrapped itself around his own in a matter of seconds, fortifying his will to live at the very least. After taking a sip of the potent concoction of the tiny animal's life, Grant made himself swallow the body completely. His body shook from the strain.

Fearful, Daniel murmured. However, as the minutes went by, he noticed some indications that Grant's body was reacting to the food. His breathing gradually slowed, and every few seconds, his eyes briefly opened.

Daniel inhaled gratefully; it's working. You're free to return home right now. I'll support you.

Not at all! Grant said with unexpected vigour.

Daniel drew back, wounded. You must! How come you won't accompany me?

They believe that me dead. Permit them. Right now I was unable to fight him.

Who will you fight? What topic are you discussing?

Daniel, consider Grant gave a sharp rebuke. The leader of the northern pack is Helmut. How on earth could he be doing this?

The plot revealed itself to Daniel, and he reeled. Francine had already attempted to bring the packs together once, but if she believed Grant was no longer there...

Daniel realised that no one could challenge him.

You Grant uttered a silent statement. You may put him to the test.

How come? Me? No, Grant. I am unable to. You made the statement yourself. I'm not an alpha.

Grant gave a heavy sigh. Daniel, you were destined to be Alpha. You are aware of it. Francine pulled me in since she knew it as well. No way her cub could have succeeded.

Daniel considered the idea. He felt the support of Grant enveloping him like a warm wave, and he took courage from it.

He freely said, "That's why she hates me." She believes that I betrayed Crane's love to Riddick.

Grant answered, "It's probably something like that." However, widows—that agony is inconceivable. To having your partner stolen from you... She's gone too far, in my opinion. Daniel, don't misunderstand: she will stop at nothing to fulfil her willingness to do this. It could end up being... She might need to be put down.

Daniel flinched at the idea. She had never been a perfect mother to him, but she was still his mother figure. A mountain of recollections from his early years fell upon him. Fish thrown to him by Francine in the river. Francine reluctantly orders Riddick to reveal his prey. Crane drew him to his side, his gold flashing eyes studying him aggressively.

Grant, though, was his mate. Abruptly, the love he felt washed away his caution and worry the way the sun erases gloom. No matter how close the threat, he would stop at nothing to protect his mate and the rest of his pack.

Daniel nosed the surviving hare towards his Alpha's muzzle as the sun started to burn off the fog, and he gently licked him until he started to eat. Then, with the weight of what he was about to do hanging over him, he crawled back out of the cave and started to jog towards home.

***

Daniel followed a meandering trail back, pausing at the location of the buck's kill in an attempt to make sense of the interactions between the scents that persisted in the clearing. Grant felt the razor-sharp tang of his blood cutting through his senses, almost overwhelming him. Putting aside his growing fury, he followed the trails to the culvert. They turned around, suggesting a deliberate scheme to hide what they had done. Grant was correct: Francine had gone too far.

When he arrived at his little home at the edge of the pine grove, it was almost midday. A mist of bacon enveloped his little garden plot, and he smiled, even at his own expense.

"Do you feel better?" he yelled from the doorway as he moved elegantly inside and took an old pair of pants from the line next to the entrance. He smiled and pointed out that the broken pieces of mirror were gone.

Gazing out of the small kitchen, Tabitha raised her head. She asked sharply, "Do you know what a pain in the ass it is to cook bacon with one arm?"

He sarcastically replied, "Gee, I'm sorry." "I'll let you go lame the next time."

"That's correct," she sighed. Feel free to eat here, you huge softie.

Daniel surveyed the living area appraisingly before making his way to the kitchen counter. Everything appeared neat and tidy, more so than it had ever been. Perched on the wooden stool, he gazed at the plate she had laid out for him, which was piled high with potatoes, eggs, and bacon.

He laughed, "You really would have been an awesome mate."

She chuckled, "Oh please shut up and eat." "And, hold on, what's that smell? Is that the case? Her eyes widened as she leaned in close to smell him. Is that a rabbit? Grant, too? Have you managed to locate Grant? Is he alright?

Daniel shook his head, trying not to show how wary he was. "Don't I constantly smell like Grant? However, yes... I chose to remove the two hares that I heard this morning digging up the comfrey. I thought it would be best to have the herbs on hand in case you end up being so mishap-prone.

"Oh, ha haha," she remarked mockingly. "Mister Big Strong Wolf Man, I had no idea you would eat a rabbit."

"Yeah, right! I simply stuffed my face down the hole while wriggling my ass in the air, acting like I was you.

With a look of heightened shock, Tabitha opened her jaws and swatted at him with the closest spatula. With his arms folded over his head, Daniel parried strike after blow while chuckling at the taste of crispy potatoes.

"Cease! Give up! I'm having dinner here, he protested.

Tabitha let out a big sigh and padded out to the restroom after making a few more pantomime threats with the spatula. Daniel laughed, more than thankful that after just one night of sleep, she had recovered so astonishingly.

He prayed in silence, "Thank you, supernatural werewolf healing abilities."

"Hey, but are you sure you've seen Grant?" Leaning in the doorway and holding a toothbrush in her mouth, Tabitha called from the bathroom.

Is that, well, my toothbrush?

With a shrug, she left through the door.

He yelled, shaking his head angrily, "No." "Has he stopped by here?"

With a spit sound and the sound of the tap being turned on, Tabitha exclaimed, "Nope!"

Daniel walked aimlessly around the room. Although Tabitha was preoccupied with her own happiness, he was worried that if she probed him too much, he wouldn't be able to convince her wolf of the truth for too long.

She reappeared and said, "Oh hey did you get the word that Francine wants us all back at the cabin?"

Daniel motioned for her to approach so he could have a better look at her plasters.

Section Two

Caster Grant pulled out his cell phone, reached up to his ear, and dialled Nigel Bennett. "Nigel, tell me you have him. Alright. In the garage, I will personally greet him. Make breakfast. After putting down his phone, he reclined in his chair. He had fashioned the plain wooden chair himself out of oak trees that grew just next to his building in the nature reserve.

He had an Olympic-sized swimming pool buried below ground, a private dinner hall on the first floor, a penthouse that occupied the top two stories, and a plethora of other amenities and diversion. Even yet, Caster Grant preferred to spend most of his time in his hidden cottage tucked away in the dense woodland of the nature reserve, even if Grant Tower contained everything he could possibly need. It was only accessible by foot, or at most by motorcycle. The path there was basically a straightforward hiking trail that wound through the woodland until it reached a meadow clearing where Caster's basic cottage was constructed. The path was neither paved nor even gravelled.

The cottage was constructed in a charming Old Dutch style, drawing inspiration from the homes he had loved as a small child. The majority of the furniture was custom-built, and the interior was earthy and rustic. It stood in sharp contrast to Grant Tower's elegant, contemporary construction.

Leids, Simon. Caster had been startled into reality by Simon's arrival in the late evening. He had been waiting years for the birth of an omega to trigger another such presence in his psychic eye. The other alphas must have been aware of the new omega's presence and would have started searching for him right away. It indicated that all of your children would be born as alphas if you mated with an omega. It was more than simply a status symbol. It denoted authority.

Caster despatched his best man, Nigel Bennett, to rescue Simon after using his wealth and contacts to locate him. Then, in an attempt to de-stress before the omega arrived, he had gone outside to his cottage.

He'd tried and failed to win over the last two omegas who'd entered his life. He had let them get away from him, but Simon would not.

"What's wrong with me?" he had questioned Nigel. "I have wealth. strong. I could offer them any kind of life they wanted.

His helper had just smiled, that knowing look he usually seemed to have, he recalled. Maybe that's not all there is to it, sir. Nigel stated.

Caster was aware of his lack of charisma. He struck the ball forcefully. He wasn't a dapper in appearance or demeanour like Nigel was. Caster was short and grumpy. He desired things to be concise and instantly to his satisfaction. Maybe it was because of his upbringing. Considering that he had never had a mother...

Caster exited into the crisp morning air after taking off his clothing and hanging them up. The home was surrounded by a gentle fog, and the early morning light gave everything a soft blue tint. He changed shape, his muscular body transforming into a formidable alpha wolf. With all speed, he shot into the forest, heading for his residence, which resembled a prison spire.

***

Caster motioned to the enormous breakfast that was arranged on the enormous table in front of them, saying, "Come, eat." Nigel stood with his arms crossed behind him in the corner. He regarded his boss sternly. Caster hurriedly added, "Please," attempting to recall his manners.

Simon was seated across from him, and because of the size of the table, he appeared little and distant. Caster looked at him, his thoughts instantly going to unsavory places. Take a look at his trim figure, he thought. I could use my cock to break him in two. Looking a little apprehensive and awkward, Simon took a fat piece of crispy charred bacon off a serving dish and put it on his plate, cutting into it without making a sound. Caster observed Simon consuming a portion. He licked off a piece of bacon that had adhered to his lips. But Caster, I wonder how that small tongue would feel on my dick.

Caster remarked sternly, "I will show you your room here after breakfast." "You will take up your responsibilities as my omega right now."

"What's my job?" Simon asked. "I didn't come here to work for you; I came here hoping to receive some answers. I've shown enough patience, you see. What the hell is going on, I want to know. and quickly, as I have to leave for work."

"I've informed your employer about your resignation already," Caster stated bluntly as he chewed into a sausage.

"What did you do?" stated Simon. What the fuck is going on here, Jesus Christ? I'm bitten by a guy, I can't stop thinking about guys, and werewolves are kidnapping me, what might be going on? And my job is gone? Could someone please explain to me what the fuck is happening?

Caster could feel his irritation building within of him. Just as he opened his mouth to calm the tiny whelp, Nigel moved closer, shot him a look, and told him to keep back if he didn't want to lose this one too. I'm sorry, Simon. I'll see to it that any doubt regarding your work is resolved, and I'll arrange for you to take the remainder of the week off to process what has transpired. We will try our best to assist you in acclimating to your new life, and Mister Grant would like to invite you to stay in his VIP suites. You are free to depart at the conclusion of the week.

Caster glanced at Nigel. Nigel merely replied with a barely noticeable grin and retreated a step. Caster scowled. In most cases, especially when it came to sensitive...emotional concerns, his helper was the expert. He gave a throat clearing. "Yes, in line with Nigel."

After Nigel's intervention, Simon appeared to be a little more composed. "All right.A week.

After fastening my belt, I examined the pockets. The tiny laser cutter, the incredibly thin climbing rope, and the decoding modules were all there. I grinned as I looked out my apartment's little, dirty window. It was a gloomy evening. Any light coming from the stars or moon was obscured by the clouds that hung near to the city. However, the city never experienced true darkness—at least not the terrifying, pitch-black darkness of the countryside. No, the city's blackness was accentuated by neon signs or brilliant artificial lighting. The fake blue-white suns and vibrant colors of the streetlamps created a cozy, welcoming atmosphere in the shadows. Naturally, there was still enough darkness for my needs.

Even the streets were silent. With hours to sunrise, it was just after midnight. The typical evening crowd had long since left for home. It was almost time for even the self-described night owls to go. Individuals were already rushing from nightclubs or bars back home. It was a private hour, just the two of us and me.

I made my way through my apartment's slackly furniture arrangement and made my way to the entrance. As I was leaving, I glanced at the mirror once and smiled at it. For comfort, I was dressed entirely in form-fitting black clothing, but I did enjoy how it emphasized my figure. Or one of my forms, anyway. From behind a mop of black hair, green eyes glinted back at me when I looked in the mirror. My pointy ears, sharp teeth, and strangely brilliant eyes hardly caught notice in such a bustling and diverse metropolis. How I wish they knew what I was concealing. Yes, I saw that both men and women would often give me a second look as I went by, but I realized that this was not a sign of distrust. People was drawn to my svelte, flexible figure and my feline grace for some reason.

I shut my door behind me as I walked out. I didn't bother locking it, ever. I was aware that if someone were to take from me, I might return the favor. That was the only two times I had to do it before word got out. In general, nobody even made another attempt. Every now and again a fresh start would think it would be a smart idea to get notoriety by robbing the notorious SymonGatt's home, but they too quickly discovered that this was not a smart move. Nobody else ventured. That was power, in my opinion.

Even as fall got closer, the city remained warm thanks to the cloud cover. I felt happy. I detested the arrival of snow and chilly winds that accompanied winter. Then the labyrinth of buildings and walls itself seemed cold and unwelcoming. But for now, I owned the city.

I walked at a leisurely pace, letting my legs spread wide. Tonight was not a rush. My sole task was to pilfer a ring from an upscale address uptown, which was so fancy that it had a house name, The Elms, instead of a number, as if the city still contained any native trees. However, Sir Reginald Charr, the mark, seemed like the kind of man who would have an antique-filled home. I laughed. Really not my type of person, but definitely my kind of mark. Individuals with such kind of attitude were usually simple to fool but too conceited to be socialized with. Not that my client was much better, but I never judged people based on how much they paid me, and this client was paying me almost too much. However, romantic disputes usually resulted in favorable results.

Walking through the streets, I had no trouble dodging the police. I'd always had keen hearing, and when I heard something unfamiliar, like footsteps, my ears would tingle. I could escape into a side-street before anyone chance to spot me. The lanes of the slums, regarded by some to be a maze, were my home, and I used that all to my advantage.

Before long, I was making my way through the wealthier area of town's wider, tree-lined streets. In fact, I greatly loved the packed, busy slums. It was more difficult to move about and conceal oneself here. That deterred many would-be thieves. I grinned as I considered that. Having the courage to try was sometimes all that was necessary to succeed. That and a little genetic assistance, anyway.

I once walked past the target residence in a hurry, with my head down. The mansion was one of the most luxurious ones, complete with gardens and an own security wall. As I passed, my eyes darted around to examine it. My extraordinary eyes were able to identify the guard seated in his small security booth between the front door and the gate, even in the dark and from the street. I didn't want to offer him anything to be excited about, but he seemed bored. Rather, I continued to stroll past the house. Between the wall of this home and the next was a small lane. I slunk between the two, taking one quick glance around to make sure no one was observing me.

I decided to take a chance since the street's few sounds had subsided by this point. Made of smooth, featureless stone, the wall must have stood eight feet tall. It was impossible to climb. I felt the muscles in my powerful legs tensing beneath me as I knelt. I jumped. With just a tiny assistance from my hand, I leaped straight onto the wall and landed in a composed, prepared position. I clenched my shoulders and lightly clutched the wall between my feet in case I had to move swiftly again. My eyes failed to detect any shadowy forms lurking, so I relaxed a little. I grinned. A wall appeared to be a real obstacle to some folks.

I lifted my head lazily and looked about the structure. I had never bothered to research other architectural styles. All I knew was whether or whether it was easy or difficult to climb buildings. With its smooth façade and multiple levels, this one was undoubtedly in the "harder to climb" category. Harder, but not impossible. There were a few enticing windows close to the ground, but I was wise enough not to fall for it. In his warnings, my client had been extremely specific. The building was familiar to him as only an ex-occupant could. All in all, though, it indicated that windows were out of the question because the bottom floor appeared to be guarded and alarmed while the above floors were only alarmed.

I pulled a climbing rope and hook out of my pack with my delicate, nimble fingers. I prepared it by mentally calculating the angle with great care. With a whistling sound through my fingers, my arm flew forth.

With a soft thud, the hook tapped softly against the wall before falling short and hitting the ground. I swore silently and pulled it back in. The hook shot up even higher on my second attempt, landing on the roof. I pulled, feeling the line tighten against a solid object. Grinning, I threw my gloved hand around the rope and jumped from the wall. I turned on the rope and sailed through the darkness, feeling the wind briefly brush against my face. With the faintest of taps, my feet hit the building's side, and I began to climb.

"Do you have any experience, kid?" said the weary-looking man behind the bar, glancing at the brief resume that Robbie had given him with excitement.

"I've had pub jobs in Sydney!" Robbie gave a perky reply.

Gay bars, the man enquired.

"Yes," Robbie nodded.

"Drag shows at gay bars?" the man pushed back.

Yes, "I was a Darlinghurst resident," Robbie answered.

The man moaned, "I have no idea where that is, but it sounds pretty and sunny and sickeningly similar to you." He sighed again and took another look at Robbie. "All right, come in tomorrow for a trial shift and let's see how you do."

"Very good!" exclaimed Robbie as he extended his hand to shake hands.

"Hello, I'm Victor," the man said, accepting Robbie's outstretched hand with caution. "This place is run by me. Show up at seven o'clock. should dress in something that is easily removed; if you want to receive some pointers, you will need to expose some skin.

*****

Robbie was leaving the pub, and the rain was falling heavily. The Rusty Nail was the name of the pub, according to the sign atop the structure.

Robbie gathered his coat snugly around himself and hurried through the downpour. There was a determined smile on his face and a bounce in his stride despite the dreadful weather. Since arriving in London a few weeks ago, he has been searching for work, and he felt as though he had made some progress recently.

This was Hackney Road in the east end of London. One of the many parts of London destroyed by the bombing raids during World War II, it was now a community dominated by council estate housing and small businesses. Robbie strolled by Turkish convenience stores, electronics stores and halal butchers, splattering through puddles on the uneven sidewalk. Even though the streets were crowded, nobody was focusing on Robbie; instead, they were all preoccupied with their own concerns. Eager to tell her about her wonderful news, Robbie was on his way home—or at least his temporary home.

Before venturing too far inside the home, Robbie shook off as much rain as he could and closed the door behind him. "Any luck?" yelled a voice from inside. It was Jason, his cousin's voice. Robbie had landed on Jason's sofa a few weeks prior when he first arrived in London. His backpack had been strewn all over Jason's living room floor, and Robbie hoped that Jason's roommates wouldn't complain too much.

"I think I got a job," Robbie exclaimed, beaming as he discovered Jason in the kitchen. "Break out the champagne."

Jason said, "Congratulations! Unfortunately, I guess we're all out of champagne. Would a cup of tea do just fine?

"It sounds like the perfect cup of tea," Robbie grinned.

With his shirt sleeves rolled up, his suit jacket hung across the back of a kitchen chair, and his tie loose around his neck, Jason remarked, "So where's the job?" while occupied with boiling the kettle.

"Yes, tomorrow is just a trial shift, but how can they not hire me once they see me in action?" Robbie shrugged. It's at a homosexual bar a few blocks away from here. Do you know about the Rusty Nail?

"Yes, indeed... The Rusty Nail gave Jason a nod.

Robbie questioned, "Why do you say it like that?" "What's the issue with it?"

"Nah!" objected Jason. "I stayed silent... I was merely restating what you mentioned. "The Rusty Nail"

"Jason," Robbie insisted.

"Oh, it's nothing," Jason shrugged. "It's just that the drag queens that perform there intimidate me a little bit, and that kind of place always seems to draw a bit of a dark, weird, and sexy crowd."

Robbie laughed and said, "Since when have you been intimidated by drag queens?"

"You know it's ridiculous, don't you?" chuckled Jason. Simply put, they are really cool, edgy, and full-on. Everything is extremely East London.

Robbie shot back, "Don't be ridiculous—you live in East London!" "You can definitely be edgy, right?"

It's like high school—those are the nice kids I want to sit next to at lunch, but they never seem to have a spot for me. You know what I mean? groaned Jason.

Robbie exclaimed with confidence, "Don't worry, my fabulously edgy cousin. Once I start working there, you'll be a regular and those cool, edgy, East London drag queens will be worshipping you!"

Jason laughed and said, "Well, let's not get our hopes up!" "It's not a huge deal; having a reason to visit there will be helpful—I hear their shows are pretty good."

"That sounds like a lot of fun!" smiled Robbie. "How was the day's work going? Have you rescued any innocent individuals from the tight grip of the law? I protest! Overruled!

Jason groaned, "You know I'm not that kind of lawyer, but work was okay. I made a significant contribution to the profits of a large bank, which I will share with my grandchildren.

"Well, even though you have sold your soul to the devil of corporate greed, I'm proud of you," grinned Robbie. I know, how about I make you dinner to commemorate starting my new job?

Jason softly said, "Um, how about I take you out for dinner instead?"

Robbie said, "Come on, I love to cook! I can cook all kinds of things!" Do you recall the cake I made for you a few years ago?

"I agree," Jason said, "which is why I'm insisting on taking you out to dinner. It's just one of the Vietnamese restaurants nearby, nothing special.

"But I," Robbie started.

"No arguments," Jason urged. "Case ended your privilege!"

"All right, then," Robbie grinned. "Please, I'm getting hungry!"

Printed in the USA
CPSIA information can be obtained
at www.ICGtesting.com
LVHW020637171223
766616LV00004B/375

9 781835 732243